LET'S LEARN ADJECTIVES!

PURPLE!

BY KATE MIKOLEY

Gareth Stevens
PUBLISHING

Please visit our website, www.garethstevens.com. For a free color catalog of all our high-quality books, call toll free 1-800-542-2595 or fax 1-877-542-2596.

Library of Congress Cataloging-in-Publication Data

Names: Mikoley, Kate, author.
Title: Let's learn adjectives! / Kate Mikoley.
Description: New York : Gareth Stevens Publishing, [2019] | Series: Wonderful world of words | Includes index.
Identifiers: LCCN 2017054282| ISBN 9781538218792 (library bound) | ISBN 9781538218815 (pbk.) | ISBN 9781538218822 (6 pack)
Subjects: LCSH: English language–Adjective. | English language–Grammar.
Classification: LCC PE1241 .M35 2018 | DDC 425/.5–dc23 LC record available at https://lccn.loc.gov/2017054282

Published in 2019 by
Gareth Stevens Publishing
111 East 14th Street, Suite 349
New York, NY 10003

Designer: Katelyn E. Reynolds
Editor: Emily Mahoney

Photo credits: Cover, pp. 1, 13 Roxana Bashyrova/Shutterstock.com; p. 5 (cheetah) JonathanC Photography/Shutterstock.com; p. 5 (ferris wheel) snowturtle/Shutterstock.com; p. 5 (girl) Radharani/Shutterstock.com; p. 7 Jess Wealleans/Shutterstock.com; p. 9 Pigprox/Shutterstock.com; p. 11 (green apples) paffy/Shutterstock.com; p. 11 (red apples) Tomo Jesenicnik/Shutterstock.com; p. 15 Chinnapong/Shutterstock.com; p. 17 Smolina Marianna/Shutterstock.com; p. 19 DiKiYaqua/Shutterstock.com; p. 21 wavebreakmedia/Shutterstock.com.

Printed in the United States of America

CPSIA compliance information: Batch #CS18GS: For further information contact Gareth Stevens, New York, New York at 1-800-542-2595.

CONTENTS

Boldface words appear in the glossary.

Descriptive Words

Adjectives are words that **describe** nouns or pronouns. They help us learn more about the other words in a sentence. This book will help you answer questions about adjectives. Be sure to check your answers on page 22!

FAST

COLORFUL

SLEEPY

5

Nouns and Pronouns

To understand what an adjective is, we first need to know what nouns and pronouns are. A noun is a person, place, or thing. Pronouns are words, such as *she* or *they*, used in place of nouns.

What furry noun is on the next page?

Awesome Adjectives

Adjectives tell us more about a noun or pronoun. For example, maybe your dad works in a building with many floors. You could say he works in a tall building. *Building* is a noun. *Tall* is an adjective that tells us about the building.

Adjectives can also help us spot differences between things that seem **similar**. Colors can be helpful adjectives for this.

What adjective could help someone understand that you're talking about the apples on the left side of the next page?

What if you had to tell someone how to find your house? There are many houses, so describing yours with an adjective can help. It's easier to find something if you know more about it.

Which word is the adjective in the phrase "the red house?"

Sizing It Up

Adjectives can also describe the size of something. Some adjectives that show size are: *big, small, tall, short, large,* and *tiny.*

Would you use the adjective *big* or *small* to describe the plant on the next page?

Some adjectives describe different levels of something. For example, if an object is really big, you could say it's big, but **gigantic** might describe it better.

If a ladybug is very small, which adjective would best describe it: *little* or *tiny?*

What's Up with Weather?

Everything can be described with adjectives, even the weather. *Hot, cold, cloudy,* and *windy* are just a few examples of adjectives we use to talk about the weather outside.

Which weather adjective would describe the sky on the next page?

Describe Yourself!

Adjectives can also describe a person's feelings or **personality**. *Happy* and *sad* are adjectives that describe someone's feelings. *Helpful* and *brave* could describe someone's personality. What adjectives could you use to describe yourself? You can make a list!

GLOSSARY

describe: to tell what something or someone is like

gigantic: very, very large

personality: the ways someone acts and feels that makes them different from other people

phrase: a group of words that tells an idea, but does not usually form a complete sentence

similar: almost the same

ANSWER KEY

p. 6: dog

p. 10: green

p. 12: red

p. 14: small

p. 16: tiny

p. 18: cloudy

FOR MORE INFORMATION

BOOKS

Blaisdell, Bette. *A Hat Full of Adjectives.* North Mankato, MN: Capstone Press, 2014.

Fandel, Jennifer. *What Is an Adjective?* North Mankato, MN: Capstone Press, 2013.

Murray, Kara. *Adjectives and Adverbs.* New York, NY: PowerKids Press, 2014.

WEBSITES

The Adjective
www.chompchomp.com/terms/adjective.htm
Learn more about these descriptive words here.

Grammar Gorillas
www.funbrain.com/games/grammar-gorillas
This fun quiz helps you better understand adjectives and other parts of speech.

INDEX

24